THE
POWER
OF
"RE"

31-DAY DEVOTIONAL

BY
COACH DELORIA MICHELLE C.P.C., MA, MBA

Copyright © 2020 by Deloria Michelle Minor

All rights reserved. This book may not be reproduced or stored in whole or in part by any means without the written permission of the author except for brief quotations for the purpose of review.

ISBN: 978-1-7341262-7-3

Edited by: Christina Consolino and Melissa Long

Published by Warren Publishing
Charlotte, NC
www.warrenpublishing.net
Printed in the United States

This book is dedicated to all of you whose life experiences have left you feeling hopeless, alone, and afraid. You are feeling destitute and distraught, with no clue as to how you are going to REstart life again. The Power of "RE" devotional will REmind you that a fighter still exists in you. Now is the time to live past the REjection, the REsistance, and the REsidue of the pain. Now is your time for a total REset!

You are a REwarrior!

AWKNOWLEDGMENTS

I would like to express my warmest and most sincere gratitude to those who have encouraged, motivated, inspired, and pushed me.

Pastor Jameliah Young, you are the epitome of a Shepard after God's own heart. I publicly thank you for EVERYTHING; when I wanted to give up you pushed me and did not allow me to quit. You push me daily to birth everything inside of me as if you are birthing yourself. July 15, 2017 was lifechanging for me and a day I will never forget. I appreciate you my Pastor, my Sister, my BFF, my Accountability Partner!

To my family, my children Ne'Erica and RJ, I love you tremendously. You two are my forever loves; thank you for blessing me with my three special gifts (Makenzie, Aiden, and Anivy). To my precious mother, Ms. Bunny, and my brother Tim, thank you for your prayers and encouragement.

To all of my fellow REwarriors, thank you for tuning in every Tuesday at 7 p.m. for our Facebook live ("The Power of RE"). Thank you for encouraging me to do this work. Remember, every day is an opportunity to REstart.

I love you all immensely and I pray God's choicest blessings upon your life!

Blessings,
Coach D

FOREWORD

Sometimes life throws us "ropes" to help us through hardships. This book is one of those ropes, reminding us that even after the toughest times, life can still be rewarding. Deloria's book will guide you toward the power and REstoration that can be found, no matter how many tidal waves you have faced.

This 31-day devotional helps to break the cycle of hurt that often comes about as the result of a divorce, a break up, or a dysfunctional or abusive relationship. Each and every "RE" word provides a building block toward an entire REconstruction of your life's path and your future relationships. In order to REdirect yourself and get the most out of this book, keep an open mind as you read it and apply it to your life.

Deloria's REdirections remind us of who we are: REwarriors. Her devotional will have you singing praises while you discover the strong woman you have become as a result of your struggles. You will learn the power of positive thinking and experience mind-blowing REjuvenation with every turn of the page.

When you are in the middle of a crisis, sometimes it can be difficult to look toward the end goal. Fortunately, this book has a rhythm to it, that like a steady drum beat, makes it easy to put one foot in front of the other with every "RE" word you encounter.

If you've picked up this book, it's because you need a push, and I am telling you, this book will push you. Even still, read it! You will be reminded that no matter what you have lost, you have the ability to be REstored. I assure you that Deloria's "RE" words will help you to find the faith behind every loss and heartache.

I am proud to call myself a REwarrior and I wish the same for you. May the power of this devotional REvive you and open your shut eyes.

Yours in Christ,
Pastor Jameliah Young

> "Courage is the most important of all the virtues, because without courage you can't practice any other virtue consistently."
>
> —MAYA ANGELOU

INTRODUCTION

The *Power of "RE" 31-Day Devotional* is a simple approach to REdoing life. The mission of this book is to provide a practical way to coalesce biblical principles with *real-life* situations that have individuals feeling hopeless, worthless, and helpless.

WHAT IS THE POWER OF "RE"?

The *Power of "RE"* is not simply a devotional book; it is a ministry of encouragement and wisdom birthed by God. Sometimes in life, we find ourselves in a transitional or transformational season that REquires us to do certain things again. Thus, the book REvolves around the prefix "RE," which when added to action words means to "do again."

This small yet power-packed devotional is a great tool to REstart areas in your life that have been major challenges. This devotional is designed to speak to those who feel like all hope is lost after having endured a major blow. Hopelessness is the beginning of defeat; defeat is a state of mind after a life-changing circumstance in which a negative impact has occurred.

After reading this 31-day devotional, you will be able to REnounce the stigma that defeat produces, and you will begin to declare life, even during your storm. Each "RE" word has significant meaning and is attached to biblical principles. Philippians 4:13 says, "I can do all this through Him who gives me strength." This 31-day devotional focuses on that message and is designed to infiltrate your broken spirit and to lead you to a place of peace so that your heart and your mind are guarded in Christ Jesus, (Philippians 4:7). Thank God for His grace and for this work.

DAY 1

Psalm 139:14
"I praise You because I am fearfully and wonderfully made; Your works are wonderful, I know that full well."

THE POWER OF "RE"
REDISCOVER

Set apart and unique is what we are, a masterpiece of His workmanship. Born with purpose and placed in the earth, we were created to give God glory. But when life happens, we forget who we are and doubt the very God who created us. At that point, we believe that the only REason for our existence is to suffer. REdiscovery of our selves will bring us back to a place of acknowledging who we are because of who we serve. At times, we lose sight of who we are. Once we do so, we begin to function from a place of acceptance because we have momentarily lost sight of the real person.

As believers, we should never allow circumstances, mishaps, or people to mask who we really are. We should REmain in a place of being true and honest with ourselves at all times. As William Shakespeare wrote, "to thine own self be true."

We must stay in tune with the Spirit until the real us is always present. Living a façade is another form of deception. "But I don't want to deceive people," we might say. Yet it's not about deceiving people any more than it is about deceiving ourselves.

So now you are left in a position to REdiscover who you are, and to do that, there must be a stripping of who you thought you were. You must allow God to peel back the layers of everything that hides you and everything that masks your true identity. These layers include weights and sins that easily beset you at one point in your life. Now, you are in a place of REdiscovery, the unveiling season for some of us and the REsurrecting season for others. REdiscovery REveals the person that God created from the foundations of the earth but that no one knew. The REsurrecting season is the season when the person who you once were comes alive again.

REdiscover you, your purpose, your assignment, and your REason for surviving some of the most difficult times in your life.

Father, thank You for REdiscovery. Thank You for REminding me that I am fearfully and wonderfully made. I am now positioned to be who You have called me to be. The layers of my past and the layers of my pain will no longer mask who I am. Thank You, for now the world will meet the me they never knew.

In Jesus' name,
Amen

DAY 2

Romans 8:37

> "No, in all these things we are more than conquerors through Him who loved us."

THE POWER OF "RE"
REBOUND

Setbacks, frustrations, obstacles, challenges, lies, accusations, defamation of character. The list of things we have found ourselves or may find ourselves in a position to REbound from goes on and on. However, the most common situation to REbound from is a RElationship gone bad. Bad RElationships, failed marriages, and abusive RElationships all tend to leave men and women alike in places from which they are unable to REturn.

Oftentimes, after these experiences, we are left in positions of not wanting to trust again, which will not allow the opportunity to love and be loved once more. The stigma of the past lingers and serves as a constant REminder of the pain that failed RElationships can cause, which subsequently hinders a potential happily ever after. In order to experience our own happily ever afters and not just celebrate everyone else's, we have to first understand that our God is bigger than the hurt; He is bigger than the pain; and He is more powerful than your offender. And since we are His, we possess the same power to rise above the opposition. As children of the Most High God, we have keys.

Matthew 16:19 says, "I will give you the keys of the kingdom of heaven; and whatever you bind on earth will be bound in heaven, and whatever you loose on earth will be loosed in heaven."

In other words, we have the authority to bind up the things that have left us believing that this is the end; we have the authority to forbid them a place in our lives and to allow the kingdom rule of God to overthrow the plans of the enemy in our lives. The oldest trick of the enemy is to steal, kill, and destroy, and these setbacks are methods meant to steal our joy, kill our faith, and destroy our destiny. *But, God!* God has come so that we may have life and live it more abundantly. Listen, there is life after the pain, which is the vehicle to the promise.

REbounding after any negatively impacting, life-altering situation *is* possible. It may seem impossible in the natural order of things, but REmember all things are possible with God, (Matthew 19:26). A conqueror is one who does not accept defeat as their final outcome, one who understands that all things work together for good, (Romans 8:28). A conqueror REbounds even against life's setbacks.

To believe you can REbound is to believe you can bounce back from the hit. Not only can you bounce back, you can also live a life free of REsidue from the hardship.

Father, thank You for the grace to REbound and the ability to start again. Thank You, Lord, for making all things possible simply because I believe. Now, God, I decree and declare total victory from everything intended for my downfall. I REnounce every illegal portal of access that the enemy once had over my mind, and I speak the mind of Christ in my life. Because I am more than a conqueror, I shall REbound and REcover.

In Jesus' name,
Amen

DAY 3

Romans 12:19

"Do not take revenge, my dear friends, but leave room for God's wrath, for it is written: 'It is mine to avenge; I will repay,' says the Lord."

THE POWER OF "RE"
RETALIATE

Many think that the best REvenge to someone who has offended us is to REtaliate, to get back, to attack that person in a similar manner but with much more force and intent. But REtaliate is a word we can bring new meaning to. We must learn how to REspond to offensive situations in ways that are conducive to peace and order. Romans 12:19 tells us that we are not to avenge ourselves but rather give place unto wrath. "For it is written: 'It is mine to avenge; I will repay,' says the Lord."

Our REsponse should be one that positively counteracts the assault or attack that was against us. REsponding in the same manner will REsult in ongoing conflict.

There are various REasons for seeking REvenge or seeking to REtaliate. However, none of those REasons are legitimate enough to hope for or actively bring about another person's demise. Heartbreak is painful; people walking out of our lives is devastating; and being lied about or lied to is disappointing and hurtful. But we must REmember the words of Proverbs 25:21-22. Our goal is to heap coals of fire on our enemy's head; that's our victory as believers. Likewise, we must REmember that the tongue is a fire starter. James 3:8 calls it an unruly evil that cannot be tamed, one that is "full of deadly poison."

While being REvengeful seems like the answer in the midst of anger and hurt, it can be very costly. The best way to seek REvenge is on your knees. "Bless those who curse you and pray for those who mistreat you," (Luke 6:28). REmember that vengeance is God's, but the victory is yours.

Father, help me to RElease the pain from the hurt,
and help me not to seek REvenge but to
seek Your face. I desire to walk in love even
when I am not loved because You are love.
Thank You for REstoring Your character in my life
and dealing with my enemies accordingly.

In Jesus' name,
Amen

DAY 4

Genesis 12:1-2

> "The Lord had said to Abram, 'Go from your country, your people, and your father's household to the land I will show you. I will make you into a great nation, and I will bless you; I will make your name great, and you will be a blessing.'"

THE POWER OF "RE"
RELOCATE

Oftentimes, we become comfortable and complacent in a particular location, position, or state of being. Becoming comfortable can hinder growth and potentially cause us to miss out on blessings we would not otherwise REceive unless there is movement away from our current state.

Familiarity is the primary REason many are content with living mediocre lifestyles and never experiencing better. Familiarity breeds contempt; contempt makes individuals feel worthless and undeserving. Once we are acclimated with contempt, we feel overwhelmed by that state of being. To settle in the state of contempt is to act out in disobedience.

In Genesis 12:1, the Lord told Abram to "Go from your country, your people and your father's household to the land I will show you." Abram did not know where he was going; all he knew was that God had spoken to him. He did not have a dialogue concerning the event, but he acted on the command and moved. Romans 4:20 tells us that Abram "did not waver through unbelief REgarding the promise of

God, but was strengthened in his faith and gave glory to God." A blessing arose from Abram's obedience; God gave him the land before him as an inheritance.

An inheritance may arise from your obedience if God asks you to RElocate and move. You may not understand His will, but you must obey His will.

Father, give me the courage I need to make this move.
Because I do not know what is before me,
and because I do not completely understand
why You are telling me to RElocate, I have
procrastinated and disobeyed. I ask now for
forgiveness, and I seek now to fully obey Your will
concerning me. I decree that this move is my setup
for greatness, and I will not fail. Now, Father,
take me by my hand and lead me to my inheritance.

In Jesus' name,
Amen

DAY 5

Exodus 6:28-30

"Now when the Lord spoke to Moses in Egypt, He said to him, 'I am the Lord. Tell Pharaoh king of Egypt everything I tell you.' But Moses said to the Lord, 'Since I speak with faltering lips, why would Pharaoh listen to me?'"

THE POWER OF "RE"
REBUTTAL

Why is it necessary for God to contend with people He is trying to bless in order for them to REceive a blessing? How does one think God has to compromise with us and negotiate REquirements to REceive what He has in store? Why is there always doubt and fear when God is executing His plan in our lives? There is a song that says, "the safest place in the whole wide world is in the will of God," yet we find the will of God to be one of the most difficult things to understand. And how do we know what the will of God is? We will REcognize the will of God when peace is elusive until we act; we will REcognize the will of God when we have a strong sense of conviction. But moreover, we will REcognize the will of God because God always establishes His word, and He will help us REcognize it, (2 Corinthians 13:1).

Although God may give us an assignment we feel unqualified for, we must obey that which He commands. REmember Moses: not only a man God used but also a man who REsponded with a REbuttal when told to go and speak to the Israelites, (Exodus 3 and Exodus 4).

God granted Moses the *specific* words and showed Moses several signs so that the people would believe. But still, Moses had a REbuttal: "Pardon Your servant, Lord. Please send someone else," (Exodus 4:13).

Constant REbuttal will have us in a state of REbellion, hindering us from REceiving the intended blessing for our lives. We must stop denying our own miracles by presenting our arguments to God. The enemy presents us with many REasons why we cannot carry out the will of God: We are inadequate. We are not qualified. We will not sound good. We are not educated. We will fail. This list of excuses goes on. If we find ourselves as Moses was, giving God a REbuttal after being told what to do, then we must understand that the enemy does not want us to carry out the assignment. Breakthrough and victory follow our obedience.

Deliverance is contingent upon *you* operating as God commands. Give God your yes and not your REbuttal, and then watch the miracles, signs, and wonders that will follow.

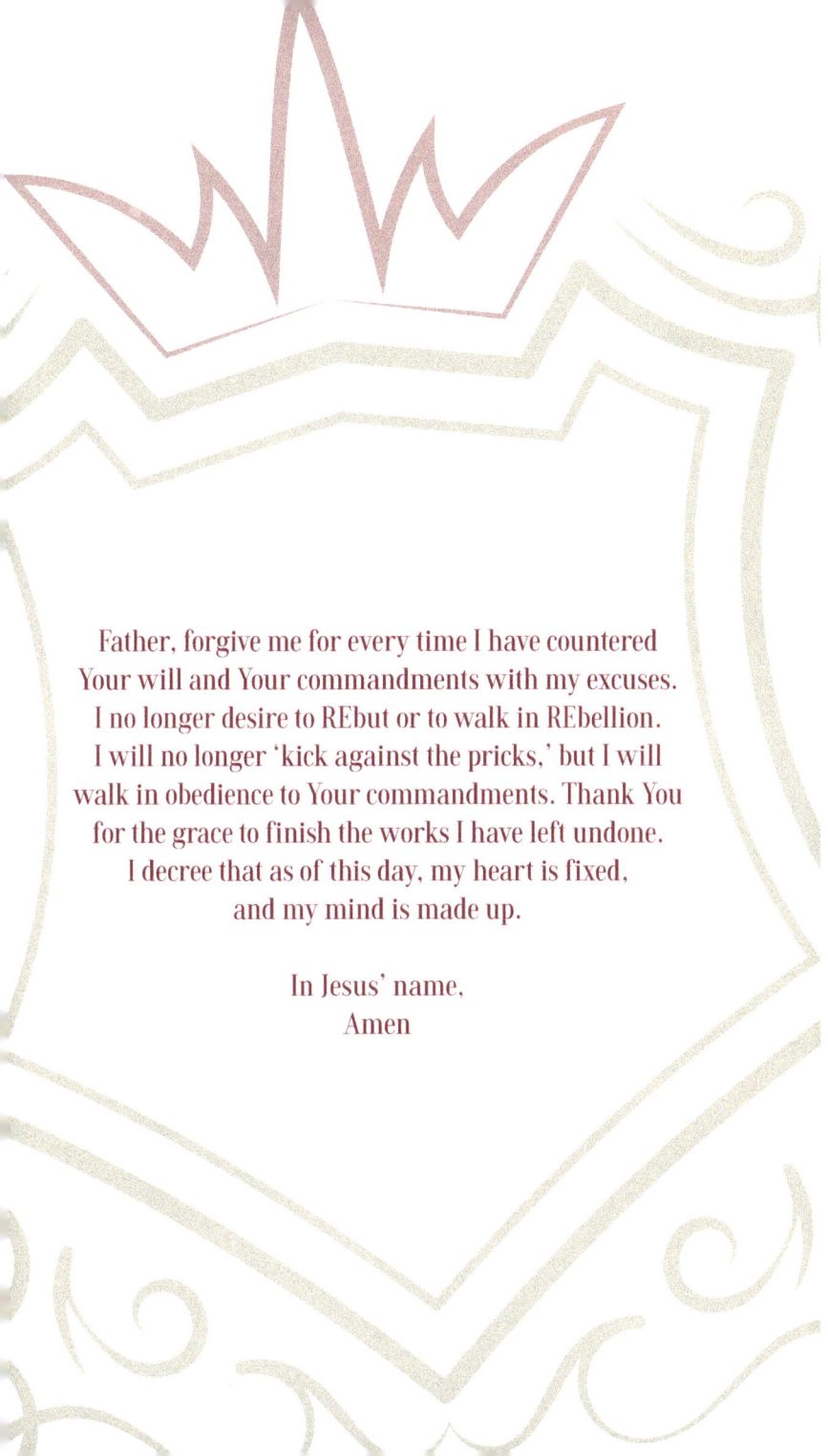

Father, forgive me for every time I have countered Your will and Your commandments with my excuses. I no longer desire to REbut or to walk in REbellion. I will no longer 'kick against the pricks,' but I will walk in obedience to Your commandments. Thank You for the grace to finish the works I have left undone. I decree that as of this day, my heart is fixed, and my mind is made up.

In Jesus' name,
Amen

DAY 6

> *Philippians 4:6*
> "Do not be anxious about anything, but in every situation, by prayer and petition, with thanksgiving, present your requests to God."

THE POWER OF "RE"
RECOVERY

Life's journey may present us with circumstances that cause us to lose things along the way. When we speak of losing things, we are not merely talking about something invaluable, insignificant, or without a purpose in our lives. We are speaking in REgard to things that are of necessity, things that are essential.

Our joy is significant; our peace is valuable; our mental sanity is necessary. The REcovery process from significant loss is not an overnight process, but we cannot become anxious while enduring the process. When anxiety sets in and things do not come together as quickly as they should, frustration mounts. And when frustration sets in, discouragement begins to settle, which can impart a strong sense of hopelessness.

At that point, we must slow down, breathe, and give our hopelessness to God. He is our master. His word tells us to be anxious for nothing and to pray in everything.

Have you tried the power of prayer in the process of REcovery? Have you made your REquest known to God? If you are not experiencing peace in the process, then you are trying to REcover alone, without the peace you REceive by following the strategy of the word:

> Do not be anxious.
> Pray in every situation.
> Be thankful.
> Present your REquests to God.

Father, I thank You for REminding me that,
in You, I am everything and I can give it all to You.
Thank You for giving me a peace in knowing there
is peace present when I make my REquests known
unto You. I decree that as I REcover, I am obedient
to Your voice. I am about to REcover more
than I lost, and for that, I am grateful.

In Jesus' name,
Amen

DAY 7

James 4:7

> "Submit yourselves, then, to God. Resist the devil, and he will flee from you."

THE POWER OF "RE"
RESIST

Most of us are familiar with the saying, "It was too good to resist." This saying indicates and validates that something in our lives affects us positively, and because of its effect, we cannot REsist it. The object that cannot be REsisted can also be a person. People with charming and strong personalities have ways of making indelible imprints on our lives. This imprint or impression leaves us in a place of desiring the company of those people even more.

The word REsist derives from the Latin word *resistere*, which means to take a stand or withstand. In order for us to operate the Power of RE in our lives, we must have a desire to REsist the familiar, anything that no longer serves a purpose but now brings pain. It can be challenging to REsist the familiar because we are content and comfortable with it.

In order to REsist that which is no longer good, we have a REsponsibility: we must submit ourselves to God. Submission to God will cause the devil and everything that is evil to flee from us. To REstart and REsist, we must submit our lives to God. A life submitted to God is no longer a life that can be controlled by anything that goes against the Word of God.

What do you have existing in your life that you need to REsist in order to operate the Power of RE and REstart your life? A bad RElationship? A bad friendship? Old habits you cannot seem to break? Whatever it is, submit yourself to God, REsist, and watch the difference God will bring to your life.

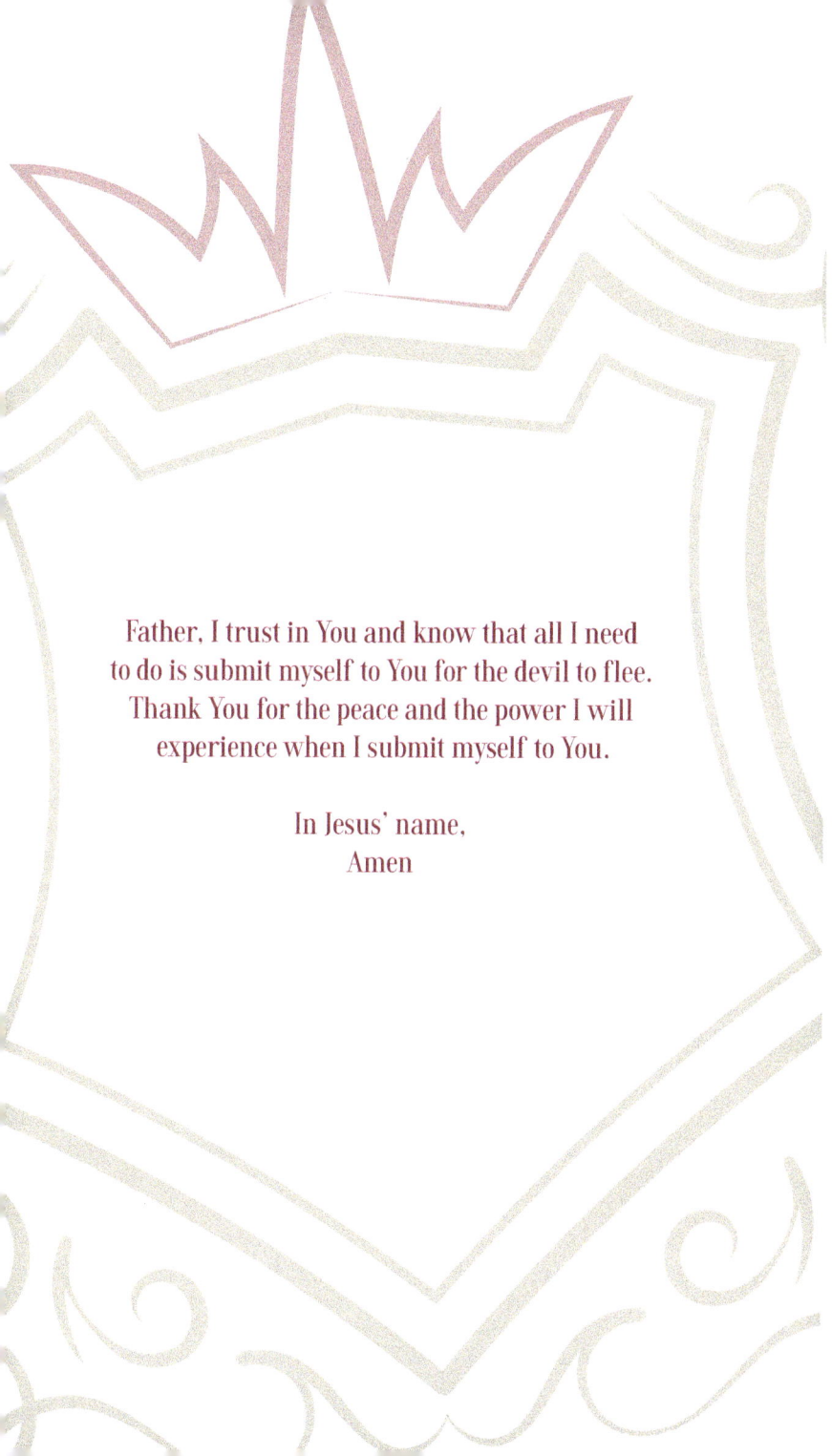

Father, I trust in You and know that all I need to do is submit myself to You for the devil to flee. Thank You for the peace and the power I will experience when I submit myself to You.

In Jesus' name,
Amen

Romans 12:2

"Do not conform to the pattern of this world, but be transformed by the renewing of your mind. Then you will be able to test and approve what God's will is — His good, pleasing, and perfect will."

THE POWER OF "RE"
RENEW

Arthur Fletcher once said, "A mind is a terrible thing to waste." While this saying suggests that it is terrible to waste brains and intelligence when one is not afforded an education, we also should not waste intelligence and energy on the past and things that cannot be changed. From the total REset perspective, keeping our minds on the things that have robbed us of peace, joy, and peace of mind would be terrible. The mind, if not REnewed, can potentially cost us everything God desires for us.

REnewing is important and something that should be practiced daily. Every day, we are faced with issues, obstacles, and challenges that can take up residence in our thoughts and affect not only the way we think but also the way in which we REspond. We must REmember that a negative thought will breed a negative REsponse. However, when the mind is REnewed in Christ Jesus, our REactions and REsponses will change.

As people of God, we should think like Christ; we should believe we are who Christ says we are, ultimately being who He has called us to be. Any mind-set opposing the will of Christ is a mind-set conformed by the world—that is to say, carnally minded. "The mind governed by the flesh is death, but the mind governed by the Spirit is life and peace. The mind governed by the flesh is hostile to God; it does not submit to God's law, nor can it do so," (Romans 8: 6-7).

The primary purpose of defeat is to distract the people of God. When we experience situations, we must REnew our mind so we can think victory in situations that bring discouragement and discontentment.

How do you REnew and maintain a spiritual mind?
1. REcognize and REnounce the source(s) of every defeating and debilitating thought.
2. REplace every defeating thought with the REfreshing Word of God.
3. Rest in what God says concerning you through His Word.
4. Rely totally on the Spirit of God to manifest the will of Christ in you.

Father God, I thank You that in all things, You have given me the victory. And now, since I know I am already victorious, I pray for my mind. I pray for the ability to REnew my mind daily, not just in the midst of adversity. I REnew my mind, and I pray the blood of Jesus over every thought. Take my thoughts captive.

In Jesus' name,
Amen

DAY 9

Luke 9:62

"No one who puts a hand to the plow and looks back is fit for service in the kingdom of God.**"**

THE POWER OF "RE"
RENEGE

REnege is a popular term some equate with the card game of spades. In this game, when a player REneges, he misplays a card that is a part of the suit being played. If discovered by the opposing team, the player's choice will cost his team several books and could potentially cost his team the whole game. In other words, by not playing the hand right, the player ultimately plays himself.

In life, when we REnege on God, the cost might be more than just a game. When we REnege on God and fail to do what God wants us to do, God says we are not fit for the kingdom. Depending on what we REnege on, we could have to pay in the form of a lifetime of unnecessary pain and trials. The Bible teaches us valuable lessons on obedience and how obedience is better than sacrifice. Even during the hardest heartbreak, the toughest trial, or the most devastating discouragement, we cannot afford to REnege on God and disobey His voice.

Yes, it's most difficult to REset after you've had your own Euroclydon experiences, but God is able. Ask yourself, am I fit for the kingdom? If the answer is no, REpent; ask

God to forgive you for REneging, and ask Him for the perseverance and the courage to stay the course. That thing you have neglected, go back and REstart it. You've come too far to stop now.

Father, forgive me for REneging on You and
not playing the hand that was dealt to me the way
I should have. Today, God, I ask for You to increase my
capacity for You. Thank You for Your word that says,
"I can do all things through Christ who strengthens
me." Lord, I love You! Thank You for loving me.

In Jesus' name,
Amen

DAY 10

Philippians 4:13
" *I can do all this through Him who gives me strength.* **"**

THE POWER OF "RE"
RETRY

How many of us have had to do something over again? How many times have we allowed a failure to make us fearful, maybe even to the point of not wanting to attempt to try again? Failure does not mean that something won't work. To REtry something after an unsuccessful attempt means we have been given an opportunity to accomplish that goal. It means we get to REtry making that goal again. Failure provides an opportunity to do something differently than we did the first time.

Maybe we have failed at trying to start a business; maybe we failed in sustaining a marriage or RElationship; or maybe we failed in switching from a lackluster career to another we passionately desired. Whatever the situation was that failed, God has given us the grace to REtry. The experience of failure does not have to be the end of anything.

One thing many do not know about me is that I have had two failed marriages. That's right! I have said "I do" twice only for both of them to end of in divorce (which REpresents failure). Will I allow two failed attempts at marriage to discourage me from ever marrying again? No,

I will not. I will take the lessons I've learned and apply them when God presents me with a new opportunity to experience a marriage (to Mr. Wonderful).

So, with every failed attempt, learn the lesson. The opportunity will present itself again. Have the mind-set that if it failed, then the time was not right. Isaiah 60:22 says, "The least of you will become a thousand, the smallest a mighty nation. I am the Lord; in its time I will do this swiftly." We must understand that destiny awaits us, but everything is according to God's timing.

REmember that you can do all things through Christ because He gives you the strength, (Philippians 4:13). Failure is not stronger than the strength of God, which REsides in you. A failed marriage, a failed business, a failed RElationship, or any other failed opportunity is weaker than the strength of God, which strengthens you.

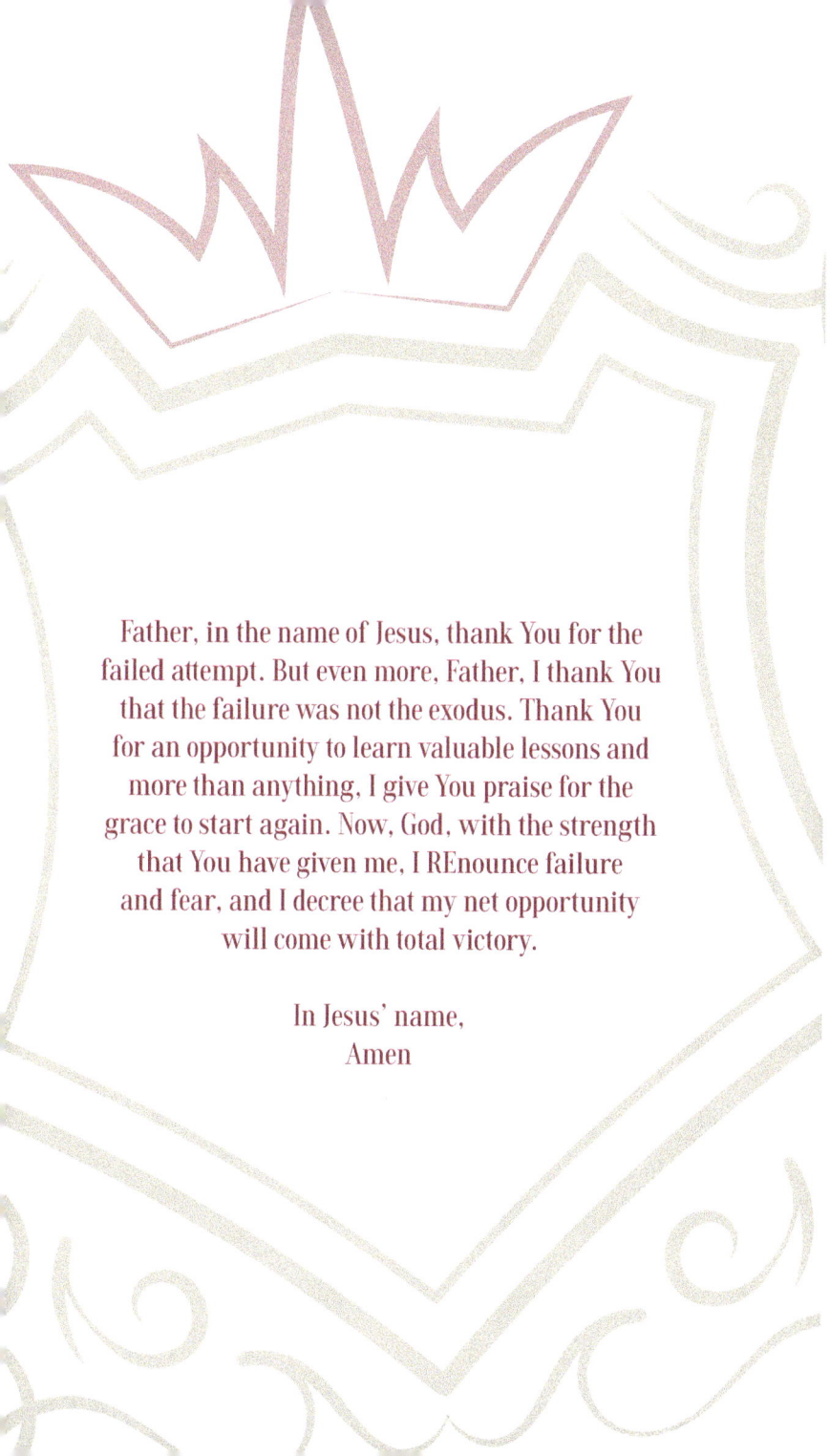

Father, in the name of Jesus, thank You for the failed attempt. But even more, Father, I thank You that the failure was not the exodus. Thank You for an opportunity to learn valuable lessons and more than anything, I give You praise for the grace to start again. Now, God, with the strength that You have given me, I REnounce failure and fear, and I decree that my net opportunity will come with total victory.

In Jesus' name,
Amen

DAY 11

Philippians 4:8

> "Finally, brothers and sisters, whatever is true, whatever is noble, whatever is right, whatever is pure, whatever is lovely, whatever is admirable—if anything is excellent or praiseworthy—think about such things."

THE POWER OF "RE"
REFOCUS

We've all experienced times in our lives when our attention needs to be directed toward what matters most. How easy is it for us to lose our focus by changing circumstances and situations that may claim our attention? The needs of our families, the demands of our jobs, and the constant hustle and bustle of life tend to grab our attention, subsequently causing us to lose our focus.

As children of God, our prayer lives and our time of being in communion with God often suffer when we are distracted. These distractions make us forget about God and His promises. The enemy, Satan himself, knows that God has a divine plan for our lives; Satan will set up opposition and devise a plan intended for our demise. As a thief, his job is to steal, kill, and destroy, (John 10:10).

When we are distracted, it is sometimes hard to REfocus our attention on what we should be doing. This inability to REfocus then places us in a cycle of REpetition, where we REpeat the same behaviors with the expectation that something different will happen. However, a change must occur in order to REceive different REsults. Change will only happen when we REfocus our attention. To REfocus is to simply REmove things out of sight that serve as blockers.

In photography, REfocusing is paramount. The photographer must REfocus the lens, bringing into view the desired subject and REmoving that which clouds the view of the subject. The photographer must have a sharp eye in order to identify the smallest detail that could potentially manipulate the image. In the Spirit, this idea is considered *discernment*.

Strong discernment is developed with a robust prayer life. When your discernment is keen, it will be hard for distractions to cause you to lose focus. Philippians 4:8 clearly states six things you should focus on; when you concentrate on these things, it will be impossible to lose focus.

Father, in the name of Jesus, thank You for Your word in Philippians 4:8 that REminds me of what I should think about. Father, I pray now that my discernment will be sharpened so that I won't be ignorant or fall prey to the devil's devices, his schemes, plots, or his plans. In the name of Jesus, I dismantle every weapon formed against me, my family, my church, and all Your children, and I cover their minds with the precious blood of Jesus.
Thank You now that I have REfocused and thank You for Your grace that is sufficient and Your mercies that are new every morning.

In Jesus' name,
Amen

DAY 12

1 John 1:9

"If we confess our sins, He is faithful and just and will forgive us our sins and purify us from all unrighteousness."

THE POWER OF "RE"
REDEDICATE

Imagine a conversation with a good friend in which she REveals something about herself; she discovered at some point, the thing in which God had blessed her and what was once considered a blessing in her life had suddenly stopped producing goodness. The happiness with which she was connected was once known as her pride and joy was no longer bringing the same pleasure and satisfaction. The very God who used to produce a harvest and sustain her by being a REsource was now drying up. Something was missing!

How do we go from prosperity and having more than enough to having just enough to get by? It doesn't seem to make sense, does it? But later, imagine that the same friend REveals a secret: the Lord spoke to her and told her to REdedicate her business back to Him.

Times like these, when God blesses us substantially and then all of a sudden, we have barely enough to sustain ourselves, REquire a REdedication back to God. Oftentimes when we are in a state of "living our best life," we tend to get comfortable with what's being produced and forget about who made it possible. We begin to unknowingly make the "thing" our god, and we fail to give glory to the all-wise God who has blessed us.

What is it in your life that needs to be REdedicated back to God? Is it a once loving and unbreakable marriage that is now in a season of chaos and confusion? Is it a business that once flourished and thrived but is now in a position of being unable to sustain itself? Is it a position you REceived without possessing the proper qualifications and credentials, and you now dread going to it? If something is no longer as it should be, it is time to step back and examine the situation. Did you begin to enjoy the fruit of what you had versus REjoicing to the God who afforded you the opportunity to enjoy what you now lack?

Whatever it is, REdedicate it back to God and watch God turn your situation around. The key to breakthrough is confession. The Bible says if we confess our sins, God is faithful to forgiveness and will cleanse us from all unrighteousness.

Father, I admit that as You blessed me,
I became more involved with enjoying the blessing
and failed to acknowledge You. I ask now for Your
forgiveness, and I now REdedicate my family, my
marriage, my job, and my business back to You.

In Jesus' name,
Amen

DAY 13

Mark 6:11
> "And if any place will not welcome you or listen to you, leave that place and shake the dust off your feet as a testimony against them."

THE POWER OF "RE"
RECEIVE

The word REceive has two ways of being perceived that are most common: to REceive something and to be REceived. We all like the feeling we have when someone REceives us (especially someone who is dear to us).

When we are REceived by others, we allow them into our personal space. We share our deepest secrets, our wildest dreams, our insecurities, and our fears. When we are REceived by others, we tend to give a little more of ourselves; we sacrifice more, and more than anything, we love hard. In other words, when we are REceived by others, we also REceive them in a way we desire to be REceived. The problem exists when we are not REceived.

Many times, we may not be REceived because people may not understand us. Some people only want to REceive us materialistically, and they are concerned with what we can do for them. They cannot REceive us as people. We must REmember that we are valuable, and we cannot allow the REjection by man to cause us to depreciate or cause us to forfeit our worth. When we are not REceived, we must learn how to RElinquish REsponsibility from an individual or a situation and move on.

The Bible tells us to "shake the dust off." In other words, wash our hands of the situation and no longer assume the REsponsibility for the truth that is not REceived. When we shake the dust off, we symbolically indicate that we have done all we can do in a situation or a RElationship. And therefore, we no longer carry it nor is there blood on our hands concerning it. We cannot allow moving on to hold us back. We must walk away free and clear, with a sense of peace in knowing we've done all we can.

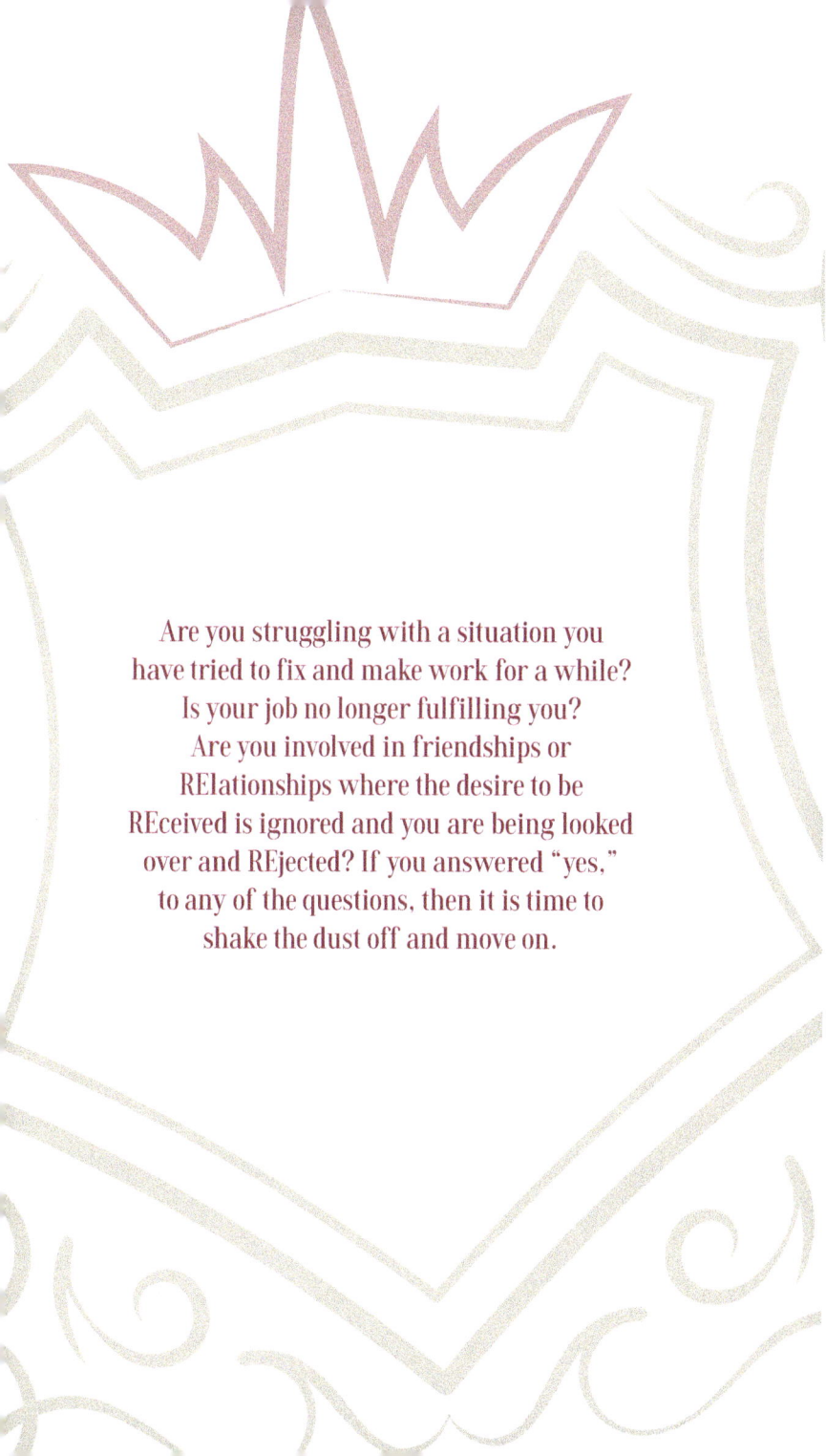

Are you struggling with a situation you have tried to fix and make work for a while? Is your job no longer fulfilling you? Are you involved in friendships or RElationships where the desire to be REceived is ignored and you are being looked over and REjected? If you answered "yes," to any of the questions, then it is time to shake the dust off and move on.

DAY 14

Ecclesiastes 9:11

"I have seen something else under the sun: The race is not to the swift or the battle to the strong, nor does food come to the wise or wealth to the brilliant or favor to the learned; but time and chance happen to them all."

THE POWER OF "RE"
REMARKABLE

Some of us need to be encouraged, to be told that what we do is remarkable and worthy of praise. *Well, what am I doing that deserves praise?* I am so glad you asked.

The fact is that we have withstood storms that would have otherwise taken us because we applied the word to the situation and stood still to see the Lord's salvation. Our actions and behavior are praiseworthy. When all hell broke loose, we exercised the fruit of the Spirit: love, joy, peace, patience, kindness, goodness, faithfulness, gentleness, and self-control, (Galatians 5:22-23).

When REtaliation seemed like the right thing to do, we REmembered the Word of God written in Romans 12:19 ("'It is mine to avenge; I will repay,' says the Lord,") and allowed God to be our avenger.

Even when we wanted to give up and throw in the towel because we thought we were inadequate for the task and did not deserve to operate in the capacity we now flow in, we REmembered the word written in Philippians 4:13, "I can do all this through Him who gives me strength."

Now is not the time to give up. There is so much on the horizon for you. Promises are about to be made and will manifest in your life. Miracles, signs, and wonders are about to follow you because you hoped against hope amid adversity. And like Abraham in Romans 4:18-22, God is going to count it unto you for righteousness. In other words, when all hope was lost and you could have given up, you fought the good fight and endured hardness as a true soldier. You endured discouragement; you endured brokenness; you suffered persecution; and you made it through your light afflictions. Now, beloved, keep pressing toward the mark for the prize of the high calling of God, (Philippians 3:14).

REmarkable!

Father, thank You for the strength and the
ability to keep going when I wanted to give up.
Thank You for equipping me for this journey
called life; and although trials may come,
I count myself as more than a conqueror,
and I declare over my life that I can do all things
through Christ who gives me the strength.

In Jesus' name,
Amen

DAY 15

Romans 12:11
> "Never be lacking in zeal, but keep your spiritual fervor, serving the Lord."

THE POWER OF "RE"
REIGNITE

Situations, circumstances, challenges, and discouragements are just a few REasons our fire for God does not burn as it should. We confess that nothing will be able to separate us from the love of God, but when things happen that shake our faith and test our belief, our fire diminishes. What a sad commentary.

Romans 12:11 tells us to never let the fire in our hearts go out. *Never* means that at no time—in the past, present, or future—should we allow the fire to extinguish. No circumstances are so powerful as to cause the fire to go out. Heartbreak and heartache seem valid enough to cause snuffing of the fire, as do divorce, family issues, broken RElationships, and other issues that challenge us on our journeys.

The fire is to be kept alive. Paul declares it best in Romans when he says nothing shall be able to separate him from the love of Christ, and in anything he should experience, he is more than a conqueror. In other words, Paul gives us hope: REgardless of what we may or may not have, REgardless of how we may be treated by others, nothing should be able to separate us from the love of Christ, and nothing should quench the fire in our hearts.

Likewise, during adverse experiences, we should see ourselves as more than conquerors, more than people who conquer, win, subdue, and overcome an adversary. Because we *are* more than conquerors; we are equipped to withstand any battle. So, when warfare rages, knowing that victory already belongs to us through Christ Jesus is enough to convince us that our fire should burn forever.

So, now it's time to REevaulate: What experiences have put out your fire? What in your life has caused your zeal to wane? Whatever *it* is, speak to it and take back what was taken from you. As you begin to speak to the hurt, the pain, the negativity, and the sufferings, you will begin to REignite the fire you once knew. And then, the power of God will permeate through the crevices of your emotional barrier; the power will conquer that which would cause you to give up and everything that would try to suffocate your fire.

Speak to your situations today and command peace amid the storm. Speak life and declare that victory belongs to Jesus.

Father, I thank You that I am able to speak Your work over my life and that the fire I once held has REignited. I thank You for the REminder that I have power over the enemy and that I am more than a conqueror. Father, forgive me for being lukewarm or even being cold in the midst of adversity. I give You all glory and honor.

In Jesus' name,
Amen

DAY 16

Isaiah 43:19

> See, I am doing a new thing! Now it springs up; do you not perceive it? I am making a way in the wilderness and streams in the wasteland.

THE POWER OF "RE"
RESIDUE

Many of us have been in places where we feel like we can go no further. Positions where we feel as though we have lost momentum. Or we feel like we have accomplished some things, but we know there is more for us to accomplish. We might be feeling like God has, just for a moment, left us. When we feel this way, it is time to REevaluate life.

Sometimes, with all that the Lord has us doing, as it pertains to our assignments and purpose, we feel as though God no longer speaks to us. That we're stuck. We do not understand why it feels like everything we're doing comes to a complete halt.

At times like this, listen to God. He will tell you that REsidue from our past causes us to pull back *after* we've been given divine momentum to *go*. The REsidue causes us to discount His power. The REsidue of our past causes fear to speak to us in a place where faith should be activated. REmember, without faith, it is impossible to please God.

REsidue is the small piece of something that still REmains after the larger portion of the object is gone. Interestingly enough, when we think about the REsidue holding us back, we are enabled to break free.

Although the RElationship may be over (the larger portion of the REsidue is gone), the voice (the small piece) still REmains. We immediately have to shake off the voice that tells us not to preach the gospel, the voice that tells us we will not amount to anything if a particular person is not in our lives. We have to shake off past failures, disappointments, hurts, shame, and ridicule and silence every voice of our past that ever spoke a negative word or was contrary to the Word of God. We cannot allow a small portion of our past to still control our lives.

You, too, must ask God to REplace the REsidue with REstoration so you can live a life pleasing to God and walk in the totality of who God created you to be. The power of your past does not and cannot supersede the power of God.

REcall the word in Isaiah 43:18–19: God said to REmember not the former, neither consider the old. He is doing a new thing in your life that is powerful enough to silence every other voice. REalize you are where you are because of His grace and mercy, and your past was only a part of your process. Ask God now to REmove the REsidue so you can continue to fulfill the assignment in your life.

Father, I thank You for the new thing You are doing in me. Yes, I perceive, and now I will walk in it. From this day forward, I decree total deliverance from the voices of my past that spoke against Your plan. Thank You, Father, for loving me enough to still use me for Your glory.

In Jesus' name,
Amen

DAY 17

Genesis 48:14

> But Israel reached out his right hand and put it on Ephraim's head, though he was the younger, and crossing his arms, he put his left hand on Manasseh's head, even though Manasseh was the firstborn.

THE POWER OF "RE"
REARRANGE

"I got *next*!" We may hear someone say that, or we may say that to ourselves, only to feel like nothing is happening. We may think everyone but us is being blessed.

When we feel this way about our lives, we should consider how God arranges and REarranges things. God will arrange a REjection to REarrange our focus. He will arrange a divine denial to REarrange our perspective. REjection does not feel good, and denials are the worst, but when the plan of God is executed, He has a way of letting us know that all things work out for our good.

Isaiah 55:8–9 teaches us about the ways and thoughts of God being higher than our ways. God's thoughts concerning us are far more than we can imagine. So, when life seemingly gets the best of us and negative thoughts plague our minds, God will show us what He thinks of us. Yes, the Bible states in Romans 12:3 that we are not to think of ourselves more highly than we ought, but what about not thinking enough of ourselves? REarrange our thoughts to think of ourselves in the ways Christ thinks. REmember that Philippians 2:5

says, "In your relationships with one another, have the same mindset as Christ Jesus."

Contrary thoughts are more detrimental to our lives than we can imagine. When we begin to think a certain way, then our behavior will begin to REflect how we think, and we will begin to act on our thoughts. That is why pulling down strongholds and casting down vain imaginations are keys to our spiritual lives and to living productive lives day-to-day.

Listen, we have all had our own personal experiences that cause our thoughts to be contrary sometimes to what God was thinking, times when what we experienced did not line up with what God spoke. James 1:2 says, "Consider it pure joy, my brothers and sisters, whenever you face trials of many kinds," which seems oxymoronic because the trials are so contradictory to the truth. In the life of a believer, it can seem as though the pressures of life are more evident in our lives than in the lives of those who do not believe. Don't worry about it; God is still God.

Be encouraged. Do not allow fear to override your faith. Just REmember, Israel crossed his hand and the blessing that would have fallen on Manasseh fell on Ephraim. You're more qualified than you think you are, and you are closer to the blessing than you know. God is REarranging things on your behalf right there in the midst of the trial.

Father, forgive me for doubting and for wavering in my faith. I know You are God, and You are working on my behalf. Thank You for REarranging things in my life to work for my good.

In Jesus' name,
Amen

DAY 18

Luke 18:1

> "Then Jesus told His disciples a parable to show them that they should always pray and not give up."

THE POWER OF "RE"
REPEAT

Persistence pays off. Often when we attempt to do something and we do not see immediate REsults, we stop what we have begun. Instead of REcognizing and valuing the lessons we should learn along the way to an accomplishment, we allow negative emotions and feelings such as discouragement and discontentment to distract us and cause us to take our eyes off that which we are attempting to accomplish. This is very true as it pertains to our prayer life. We already know that the effective, fervent prayers of the righteous avail much. But when God is seemingly taking His time concerning our REquests, we lose hope. When we lose hope, the tenacity to pray dissipates, and we stop praying. Negative circumstances should never take us out of our posture of prayer; they should keep you constant in prayer.

A lesson in Luke talks about a poor, powerless widow who nags a corrupt, powerful judge to grant justice to her. Just as this poor widow was going before a corrupt judge with her REquest, we should go to a just and loving God with our REquests. The parable here is that we should always pray and never have a faint heart. Even when faced with the most challenging circumstances or the most difficult people, we should never cease to pray and lose hope. When we are faced with challenges and difficulties, we should always persevere because of our faith.

Although the poor widow asked for justice from a corrupt judge, she did not allow who he was or his corrupt nature to stop her from presenting her REquest. Even in the face of injustice and corruption, God can bring about justice for His people. God works best in impossibilities. We have heard it so many times: He is a miracle worker and shows us signs and wonders. We have to REmember the times when we've walked with Christ and were faced with challenges. Those challenges have sometimes suddenly worked out. And not only have they worked out, but they worked out for our good.

In order for us as believers to see the constant power of God manifest in our lives, *we* must REmain constant. We must REmain constant in our praying just as the widow was constant with taking her request to a corrupt judge. We cannot change positions REgardless of the giants and the obstacles we face. We must REmain constant in our obedience, and we must REmain constant in our faith. Faith without works is dead. REmember, man's power is limited, but God's power is limitless; God has infinite power.

So now, even in the face of opposition, it's time for you to REturn to your praying position and REpeat what you have done in the past to bring about your deliverance. In going to God, you should never feel like you are a burden to Him. He tells us to cast our cares on Him for He cares for us, (1 Peter 5:7). REtain your prayer posture, and REpeat your REquests; God, our deliverer, is waiting to hear from you.

Father, thank You for the awesome privilege to come boldly to Your throne. Thank You for always granting me access to pray to You and to cast my cares on You. Thank You that no matter what I may face, You are always there, even in the midst of opposition, to turn the heart of the king and work things out for my good. I am grateful!

In Jesus' name,
Amen

DAY 19

Ephesians 5:1-2

"Follow God's example, therefore, as dearly loved children and walk in the way of love, just as Christ loved us and gave Himself up for us as a fragrant offering and sacrifice to God."

THE POWER OF "RE"
REFLECTION

Sometimes in life, we are not proud of ourselves. We might look in the mirror, not for purposes of making sure our physical appearances are on point but to deeply REflect on ourselves. For anyone who has attempted deep REflection, what was the REsult? What or who was REflected back? And were we proud of that REflection? Most of all, the greatest question is: was the REflection an imitator of Christ?

REflecting on ourselves involves facing the challenges that have made times difficult. In facing the challenges, we look at how we REsponded to those challenges and who we REpresented during those challenges. In the most difficult times, we must always REmember to be a REflection of Christ Jesus. Being a REflection of Christ is simply to take on His character. Having a REflection of Christ means being a REpresentation of the kingdom of God. The Bible teaches that we are ambassadors of Christ, (2 Corinthians 5:18-20). Therefore, our character should REflect the light of who Christ is.

REflection can be defined as a REpresentation or an effect produced by an influence. REflecting Christ is effortless when there are no challenges to contend with. REflecting Christ is easy when the marriage is good, when the job is stable, and when everything flows as it should. The test of who we truly REflect occurs when opposition presents itself. How can we REflect Christ when overwhelming situations arise?

In order to have a REflection of Christ, you must have a RElationship with Him. RElationships are strongest when time is spent with the one you are in a RElationship with. For example, strong RElationships with significant others REquire time spent together. The amount of time spent is imperative to the survival and the health of the RElationship. Furthermore, when time is spent with someone, you begin to take on their traits or their characteristics. You begin to emulate some of their behaviors. Emulating behaviors from people other than Christ can be good in a sense and not so good in another; we know there is none perfect but the Father in Heaven, (Matthew 5:48).

When you spend time with Christ and develop a RElationship with Him, you soon begin to emulate His character and become a REflection of who He is here on this earth. When you emulate Christ, He is glorified in you and through you. Your light is continually shining. Matthew 5:16 says, "In the same way, let your light shine before others, that they may see your good deeds and glorify your Father in heaven." In other words, when God is glorified in you, when you are a REflection of who He is, then He (Christ) is glorified through you.

Father, I ask now for forgiveness for every time I have been guilty of not REflecting the true character of who You are. I acknowledge that during some of the hardest times in my life, I did not emulate who You are and who You continue to be. I ask now that You would wash me in the precious blood of Your son, Jesus, and create in me a clean heart so that I can REflect Your character, Your love, and Your wisdom in all I say and do. From this day forward, my desire is that You are glorified in me.

In Jesus' name,
Amen

DAY 20

Revelation 2:4-5

"Yet I hold this against you: You have forsaken the love you had at first. Consider how far you have fallen! Repent and do the things you did at first. If you do not repent, I will come to you and remove your lampstand from its place."

THE POWER OF "RE"
REACQUAINT

Setbacks, distractions, trials, and personal agendas are all examples of life occurrences that may cause a broken fellowship or a broken RElationship with Christ. Broken fellowships are not situations we make plans for; they happen unexpectedly. Broken fellowships and broken RElationships with Christ can REsult in a turning away from Christ, which is a bad state in which to find ourselves.

When we fall out of communion with Christ, our joy is gone, it seems hard to praise and worship, and we might go through a season of not praying as we should. During these experiences, it is safe to say we need to be REacquainted with Christ and His love. We may ask, "How do we really know that we need to REacquaint ourselves?" REacquaintance is necessary if we begin to justify actions that are considered to be disobedient, if we would rather do what feels good versus what is right, or even if our worship is dry and sincerity doesn't exist behind our praise.

To REacquaint is simply to familiarize yourself with someone or something again. Some people are meant to be in your life only for a season; they have a purpose designed by God to be a part of your life, and once that purpose is fulfilled, then the RElationship is forsaken. RElationships with people and RElationships with Christ are different in the fact that a forsaken RElationship with Christ can be detrimental to your soul.

Revelations 2 reveals that seven letters were written to the seven churches, and the Church of Ephesus was the first church God addressed. The members of the Church of Ephesus were charged with losing their passion and excitement for Christ; their love for Christ was abandoned and Christ's teachings were also abandoned. God told the people He had something against them because they had forsaken their first love, (verse 4). So how were they to be REacquainted with their first love? In verse 5, they were instructed to consider (or REmember) how far they had fallen and to REpent. Like the members of the Church of Ephesus, you must consider how far you are REmoved from your first love, who is Christ; you have to consider what happened to make you lose your zeal and consider what happened to make your worship dry. Once you consider, you must REpent.

In the same way that Christ instructed the Church of Ephesus to consider and REpent in order to be REstored, you must do the same. You must consider the love Christ has for all of us and how it allows space for REpentance. REpentance is a heart change, from selfish desire to the desire to obey God. REpent today and REacquaint yourself with the love of God.

Father, in the name of Your son, Jesus, I come to You with REpentance in my heart. I am sorry for forsaking my RElationship with You. I admit I was distracted and failed to seek You while in my down moments. As Your word has instructed, I am considering my ways, and I REpent. I humbly ask to be REstored.

In Jesus' name,
Amen

DAY 21

James 1:12

> "Blessed is the one who perseveres under trial because, having stood the test, that person will receive the crown of life that the Lord has promised to those who love Him."

THE POWER OF "RE"
RESILIENCE

Trials and tests are inevitable in the lives of believers and nonbelievers alike. A thought exists, especially among new believers, that once we confess Jesus as our Lord and Savior and we have REceived Him in our hearts, we will live a trouble-free life. We must dispel that myth and cast down that very thought of living trouble-free lives. Throughout the Bible, we will learn of many tests and trials endured by followers of Christ. The encouragement in all we may read about is that endurance leads to many victories. Romans 8:28 teaches us that "in all things God works for the good of those who love Him, who have been called according to His purpose."

Although faith is necessary to please God, (Hebrews 11:6), it becomes very difficult to exercise the mustard-seed faith when we are living through and adapting to stressful life changes, hardships, and crises. Even though we experience negative, life-altering, and some life-shattering events, we somehow become able to withstand the trials and recover from the difficulties of them. We become REsilient during the trials.

Becoming REsilient or exercising REsilience is the ability to REcover or adjust easily; it is the ability purposed in our hearts to go through the suffering and do things differently. When have we exercised REsilience in our lives? A life-changing event can be very disheartening and discouraging. REsilience does not mean we are intentionally nonchalant or uncaring about a situation; it simply means, "I will REspond to my trial with an attitude that will allow me to grow and bounce back."

If we study the apostle Paul's life, we can conclude that he is the epitome of what REsilience looks like. Paul was beaten, stoned, jailed, and almost killed. Paul simply got up and continued his missionary journeys REgardless of the opposition he faced on many occasions.

Like Paul, we should become REsilient during opposition, pick ourselves up, and continue this journey called life. James 1:12 says, "Blessed is the one who perseveres under trial," and perseverance produces something far greater than the trial itself. Despite the sufferings, we must always REmember that God is in control.

REmember Job? He was considered for his trial. The Lord asked Satan in Job 1:8, "Have you considered my servant Job?" Job suffered great loss, but his perseverance paid off, and he REceived double the blessings for his trouble. REmain faithful during the trial, knowing that you shall REceive something greater when you make it through.

Father, in the name of Jesus, I thank You for
the spirit and the ability to persevere when
I am going through trials. Thank You that greater
is He that is in me than He that is in the world.
And because the greater one lives inside of me,
I decree and declare victory through every trial and
every test. I know I am more than a conqueror,
and because of that, this too shall pass.

In Jesus' name,
Amen

DAY 22

1 Samuel 1:12-14

"As she kept on praying to the Lord, Eli observed her mouth. Hannah was praying in her heart, and her lips were moving but her voice was not heard. Eli thought she was drunk and said to her, 'How long are you going to stay drunk? Put away your wine.'"

THE POWER OF "RE"
RELENTLESS

Having a clear vision includes establishing the steps needed to achieve that particular goal. In addition to following the necessary steps, something must be embedded in our spirits that allows us to move with tenacity. This embedded force allows us to never give up until we meet our objectives and celebrate the victory. REgardless of how big or small the goal is, an exceptional, extraordinary type of drive must push us forward. Becoming unstoppable and determined and having a willingness not to give up even when situations become unpleasant are all characteristics of a person who is RElentless.

RElentlessness REquires persistence and consistency. In other words, when we are in pursuit of something, there has to be a level of commitment within that is self-encouraging and self-motivating. RElentlessness says, "I will not stop until I accomplish what I have purposed in my heart to accomplish."

Hannah is an example of someone with RElentless faith. Hannah had a desire to have a child, but she was barren. However, she became unstoppable in her faith. Although the Bible never mentions the age at which Hannah was able to conceive her first son, Samuel, her rival (Peninnah) birthed ten sons and two daughters before Hannah was able to conceive. The Bible states that Hannah's rival provoked Hannah until she wept and would not eat. But Hannah did not give up. She was RElentless in her faith and poured out her soul to the Lord, (1 Samuel 1:15). Hannah's RElentless faith worked for her; persistence paid off and consistency accomplished the desire.

We can learn so much from Hannah about being RElentless. Hannah was clear about what she desired, and she did not allow any opposition or her rival to cause her to lose sight of what she desired. She knew exactly what to do and whom to call on in order to accomplish what she desired.

Maybe you are facing challenges that seem impossible, and you are ready to give up. Don't give up. Become so RElentless in your faith and pour out your desire to God, the one who will guide you until what you desire is obtained. "Take delight in the Lord, and He will give you the desires of your heart," (Psalm 37:4). Under pressure and in the midst of being provoked—even while being accused of being drunk—Hannah delighted herself in the source and was able to conceive: "And the Lord was gracious to Hannah; she gave birth to three sons and two daughters. Meanwhile, the boy Samuel grew up in the presence of the Lord," (1 Samuel 2:21).

Father, in the name of Jesus, I ask for a RElentless spirit. Lord, raise up the warrior and the conqueror in me that would cause me to see victory even in barren situations. Your word says I am more than a conqueror and I can do all things through Christ, who gives me the strength. I decree and declare from this moment on that I am RElentless in my faith. Now allow Your light to shine upon my ways to make my desires obtainable. By faith, I announce my victories and denounce my fears.

In Jesus' name,
Amen

DAY 23

Psalm 55:22-23

> Cast your cares on the Lord and He will sustain you; He will never let the righteous be shaken. But You, God, will bring down the wicked into the pit of decay; the bloodthirsty and deceitful will not live out half their days.

THE POWER OF "RE"
REDUCE

It is a wonderful thing to know that our burdens and our battles really do not belong to us. Several scriptures encourage readers to REmember that the battle belongs to God. In order for God to fight our battles and handle our burdens, we must trust Him with the things that hurt and disturb us the most. It is at these times that our understanding of God's plan and His will seems so vague and bleak, making it harder to trust. These character-building moments should intensify our faith and solidify God's authority in our lives. However, intensified faith and solidified kingdom authority is REduced because we become faint, and we lean on our own understanding.

Proverbs 3:5 says to "Trust in the Lord with all your heart and lean not on your own understanding." There is a REason for trusting and not leaning, but unfortunately, burdens sometimes cause more leaning than trusting. When we do not trust God but lean on our own understanding, the Lord cannot sustain us. Hence, we become overwhelmed and shaken in our faith, left feeling depleted and defeated. Stress and anxiety begin to settle in our spirits, leading us to believe that there is no way out of our situation or there is no hope for our case.

How do we get past the negative emotions when burdens become too heavy? REduce! REduce means to lower in condition or diminish in strength. As believers, we must learn to REduce anything that opposes the strength and power of the Word of God in our lives. The Word of God is ineffective when we fail to trust God with our *all*. God delights in the prosperity of His children, (Psalm 35:27). Our prosperity is not limited to monetary prosperity, but we are prosperous in mind, body, and spirit.

It is totally up to us if we are going to trust God (although we may not always be fruitful in our understanding) or if we are going to lean on our own understanding and REmain in a place of feeling overwhelmed while trying to work situations out alone. God has promised that He will never leave us nor will He forsake us. His ways are not our ways, and His thoughts are not our thoughts; His ways and His thoughts are higher than ours. To totally trust God means we acknowledge Him as being God when all is well, and we acknowledge Him as God even when we have battles that may overwhelm us.

REducing stress and anxiety means to diminish the strength of what you see with the natural eye and to look through the lens of the Spirit to see the power of God working and carrying you through the battle. As the spirit of the Lord spoke to Jehoshaphat and told him, "Do not be afraid or discouraged because of this vast army. For the battle is not yours but God's," (2 Chronicles 20:15). The same applies in our lives: our battles belong to God.

Father, in the name of Jesus, I ask first for forgiveness. Forgive me for REducing Your power in my life by trying to fight my battles in my own strength. I claim total dependence on You to carry me through every storm. I now cast my cares on You, knowing You will sustain me during difficult times.

In Jesus' name,
Amen

DAY 24

Luke 6:45

"A good man brings good things out of the good stored up in his heart, and an evil man brings evil things out of the evil stored up in his heart. For the mouth speaks what the heart is full of."

THE POWER OF "RE"
RECIPROCATE

The Bible teaches us that it is more blessed to give than to REceive, (Acts 20:35). But in RElationships and in friendships, how much of ourselves can we give and not REceive in return before the RElationship or friendship is deemed over? Divorce and breakups tend to happen when one party gives more than the other party in terms of love, affection, compassion, concern, and other emotional factors. The lack of these can lead to the demise of a RElationship.

Couples seek therapy because of emptiness, loneliness, and unfulfillment in a RElationship. Voids can be created because one of the individuals is not meeting the needs of the other. These voids cause a sense of neglect and can REsult in infidelity. In the simplest terms, what is given out by one is not REciprocated by the other.

The act of REciprocating is simply giving and taking mutually, REsponding to an action with a corresponding action. Although we would desire to give and REceive that which is good and edifying, there are times when bad deeds, attitudes, and mistreatments may be what is REciprocated, which can be considered REvenge. Several Scriptures demonstrate that vengeance belongs to God, and we are not to render evil for evil. However, in RElationships, friendships, marriages, and more, the mind-set is to give back what was given.

According to Luke, (6:45), what a man gives and shows toward another is what is stored up in the heart; what comes out of the mouth is what was in the heart. How many times have we REsponded in a situation and later tried to REtract what was said? Instead of thinking before REsponding, we REspond out of emotion. Our speech should always be with grace and "seasoned with salt" so that we will REspond as we ought to REspond, (Colossians 4:6).

In retrospect, how many broken RElationships have you endured because of what was REciprocated or what was not REciprocated? Forgive yourself, RElease yourself from what was, and embrace what is now. Stay open to REceiving and believe God for that moment, for your love, compassion, and goodness will be REturned.

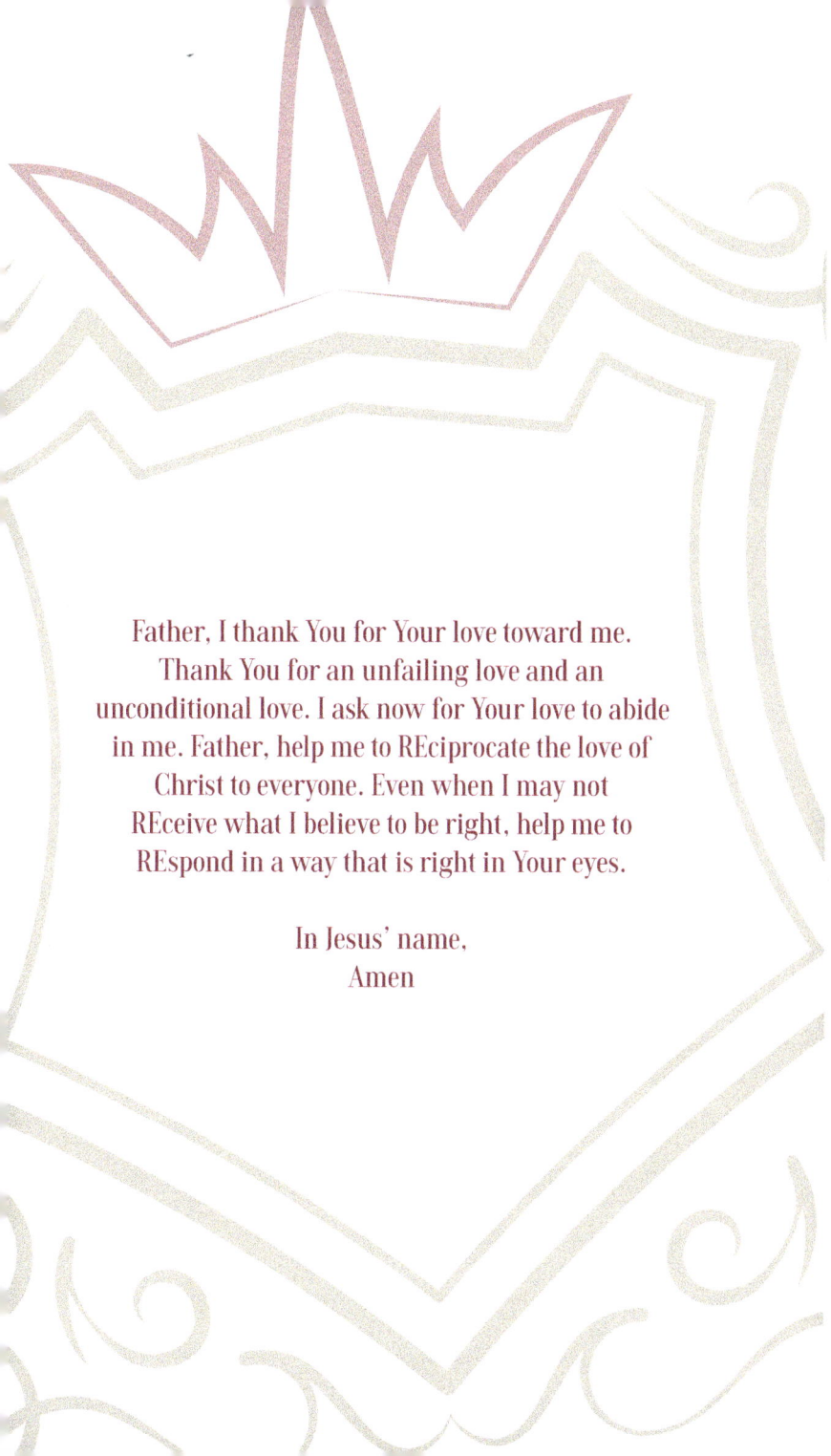

Father, I thank You for Your love toward me. Thank You for an unfailing love and an unconditional love. I ask now for Your love to abide in me. Father, help me to REciprocate the love of Christ to everyone. Even when I may not REceive what I believe to be right, help me to REspond in a way that is right in Your eyes.

In Jesus' name,
Amen

DAY 25

Psalm 118:22
"The stone the builders rejected has become the cornerstone."

THE POWER OF "RE"
REJECTION

REjection is a word we do not like to hear nor experience; it is a word that carries a heavy negative connotation, and the impact of the word can be damaging. Social REjection and RElationship REjection can cause a myriad of emotions including anxiety, depression, and sadness. REjection has the potential to leave you feeling unwanted, unworthy, and useless. REjection is especially painful when you are REjected by those you love.

Although the word carries a negative connotation, REjection can be a good thing. It can be the camouflage that keeps us from being deceived and hurt, especially in RElationships. When we are in a RElationship with someone, we expect for the person to love us as much as we love them. That is not the only expectation in a RElationship, marriage, or courtship. An expectation of mutual REspect also exists. Along with the love and mutual REspect, loyalty and honesty are desired or REquired. Unfortunately, when the expectations are not fulfilled, we are left to feel REjected.

With this in mind, when we experience REjection, a common thought arises: why would someone we love REject us? The truth of the matter is that we may never REceive an explanation as to why someone has REjected us. However, we owe it to ourselves to accept what we may never understand. Accepting REjection does not mean accepting a personality flaw within ourselves; accepting REjection is to understand that the one who REjects may have a flaw within themselves that has nothing to do with us.

Yes, in some instances people REject others because of their own insecurities. Did you ever think that someone could have a deep admiration for you to the point of making them feel unworthy of your goodness? Has it ever occurred to you that they might have a desire to do some of the wonderful, unique, and creative things you do? Or maybe they have a desire to accomplish what you have accomplished without depending on anyone else. Think about it! If you have been REjected or are being REjected and there is no apparent REason why, then you must understand that the REjection has nothing to do with you and everything to do with the person who is REjecting you. Now, it is up to you to continue to accept or to REject what is given and shake the dust off.

Although you may experience REjection, that REjection does not negate the greatness that is within you. REmember, the REjected stone became the chief cornerstone.

Father, forgive every person who has REjected me. Cleanse me from the sting of the REjection and give me a heart to still love those who have knowingly and unknowingly hurt me by the act of REjection. Lord, if I have caused others pain by REjecting them, I ask for forgiveness and please allow me the opportunity to REceive them once again.

In Jesus' name,
Amen

DAY 26

Galatians 5:24-25

"Those who belong to Christ Jesus have crucified the flesh with its passions and desires. Since we live by the Spirit, let us keep in step with the Spirit."

THE POWER OF "RE"
REPRESENT

Character and integrity are everything. Both good character and a high level of integrity are needed to sustain Christians in their walk with Christ. At the same time, a person's character speaks to whom they REpresent. To REpresent in this sense means to serve as an example. As believers and children of God, we are to serve as His examples on Earth. We are Christ's ambassadors. As ambassadors we have the REsponsibility to live a life that REpresents the character of God.

1 Thessalonians 2:4 states we have been approved by God and entrusted with the gospel, and we speak, not to please man but to please God, who tests our hearts. In other words, as an ambassador of Christ, we should REpresent Christ by our behaviors and our actions, and we must be careful to speak in a way that is pleasing to God. As REpresentatives of the kingdom, we have a REsponsibility to please God and not man.

But how do we REpresent the Most High God when our backs are against the wall? How do we REpresent the character of God when we are continuously being tested?

How is it possible to REpresent God when all around us there is evil? REpresenting Christ is a lifestyle. We REpresent Christ by how we live; we REpresent Christ by how we love; and as difficult as it might be, we REpresent Christ by how we forgive. Understand, there is no greater love than the love Christ has for us, but the greatest gift of all is love. Likewise, forgiveness has no maximum capacity. In the same way that Christ forgives us when we are wrong, we are to forgive others when they have wronged us.

REpresenting Christ and showing His character is not impossible. To REpresent Christ simply means to follow His commandments. John 14:15 states that Jesus told His disciples right before His crucifixion, "If you love me, keep my commands." When you obey Christ, you not only REpresent Him and show a dying world His character but also show obedience to His commandments and show forth your love for Him. When you love someone or something, you will REpresent them well. Just as you seek to REpresent the organizations in which you work well and make the organization a reputable one, you should REpresent the kingdom of God even more so. After all, when you REpresent Christ by obedience to His word, then great is your REward.

Father, I pray that in all I say and in all I do, I REpresent You well. Let my behavior and my conversation speak to Your character. I am Your ambassador, and I seek to REpresent You well.

In Jesus' name,
Amen

DAY 27

2 Corinthians 4:1-2

"Therefore, since through God's mercy we have this ministry, we do not lose heart. Rather, we have renounced secret and shameful ways; we do not use deception, nor do we distort the word of God. On the contrary, by setting forth the truth plainly we commend ourselves to everyone's conscience in the sight of God."

THE POWER OF "RE"
RENOUNCE

REfuse and REject! We have a right to say *no*. We have the right to REfuse and REject anything that does not compliment us. We have the right to REfuse or REject anything that does not inspire or REquire us to be better people and do greater things. We are all created with a purpose. Some of us REcognize our purpose while some may not know yet what their purpose is.

Purpose as it RElates to all of us can be defined as an intention or objective for living. God created all of us with the intention on using us to do something great and unique. There is an objective to our existence. In other words, our very existence is not in vain. On the contrary, some have suffered opposition and challenging situations for so long, it's difficult to convince them that their lives have purpose. Many are stagnant in progressing in life because of what has been. They have endured but are convinced they have no purpose.

This is far from the truth. Now is the time for us to understand that everyone has a purpose. We did not survive our storms only to live with the mentality of defeat. The fact that we survived speaks to the conquerors in us. Romans 8:37 says, "No, in all these things we are more than conquerors through Him who loved us." In other words, in all the things we were able to go through, and in all the things we have survived, we were able to conquer, subdue, and overthrow the opposition we were facing.

Since you have conquered and are victorious, now REnounce anything that will say otherwise. REnounce the shame, REnounce the embarrassment, and REnounce every negative emotion that will keep you from being better. The worst is over; it is time to follow Christ and live the life He has preordained for you.

Now is also the time to REnew your mind and put on the mind of Christ. Now is the time to walk out your purpose. The trouble you've experienced served as the vehicle of strength you needed to build your character for *this* moment. It's your moment to do great things; it's your moment to be a force to reckon with. It's your time now to live the life God has designed for you. The past is over, and the mistakes have been made. Now, REnounce everything that says life is over because life is just beginning.

Father, I thank You for where I have been, and I thank You for Your strength that allowed me to endure. Now I ask for courage to REnounce everything that would hinder me from moving forward. I REnounce every hidden thing that is designed to stunt my growth. Thank You, Father, for I am more than a conqueror because You love me.

In Jesus' name,
Amen

DAY 28

Daniel 3:12

"But there are some Jews whom you have set over the affairs of the province of Babylon—Shadrach, Meshach and Abednego—who pay no attention to you, Your Majesty. They neither serve your gods nor worship the image of gold you have set up."

THE POWER OF "RE"
REFUSE

To REfuse simply means to show an unwillingness or an aversion to accepting or granting something. Many times, when we are attempting to salvage RElationships and continue in something that is not good for us, we will act against our own will. In acting against that will, we make someone else a priority over ourselves. This type of action or behavior REsults in a very unhappy and imbalanced life.

There is absolutely nothing wrong with REfusing to comply with anything we do not have the will to do. Many have complied with others at one point or another, whether at home or in the marketplace. Some of us have adapted to a theory of "keeping the peace" by agreeing with the REasoning of another person, even when it goes against our will, which is simply not right. The hardest thing to do at times is to REfuse our loved ones or to simply say no.

But if we love ourselves and love others enough, then to REfuse something that goes against our will is the right thing to do because our lack of REfusal may later lead to a bigger consequence. In life, we know we can choose our actions, but we cannot choose our consequences. Parents know this all too well. Raising children is challenging, especially when those children simply REfuse the instructions given and disobey house rules. This leads to consequences they would not choose. Oftentimes, consequences are more severe than the REquirements of the task.

Shadrach, Meshach, and Abednego REfused to bow and worship the golden image King Nebuchadnezzar had set up. They did not comply with the king's order although everyone else around them did. They REmained true to what they believed and who they believed in. They held to their truth: God would deliver them from the furnace, but if He didn't, they would not serve the gods or worship the image. Had they not REfused, they would have compromised their truth.

To REfuse something is not a death sentence; there may be consequences, but just like the three were delivered from the fiery furnace, God can deliver you from fiery circumstances, whether they be toxic jobs, domestic violence situations, or instances where you feel forced to do something immoral. You can REfuse and trust God to deliver and bring you through.

Father, give me the strength and the courage to REfuse to do anything that is contrary to Your perfect will. Help me to guard myself by not compromising what I know is right. I present myself as a living sacrifice, and I seek to please You in all I say and do.

In Jesus' name,
Amen

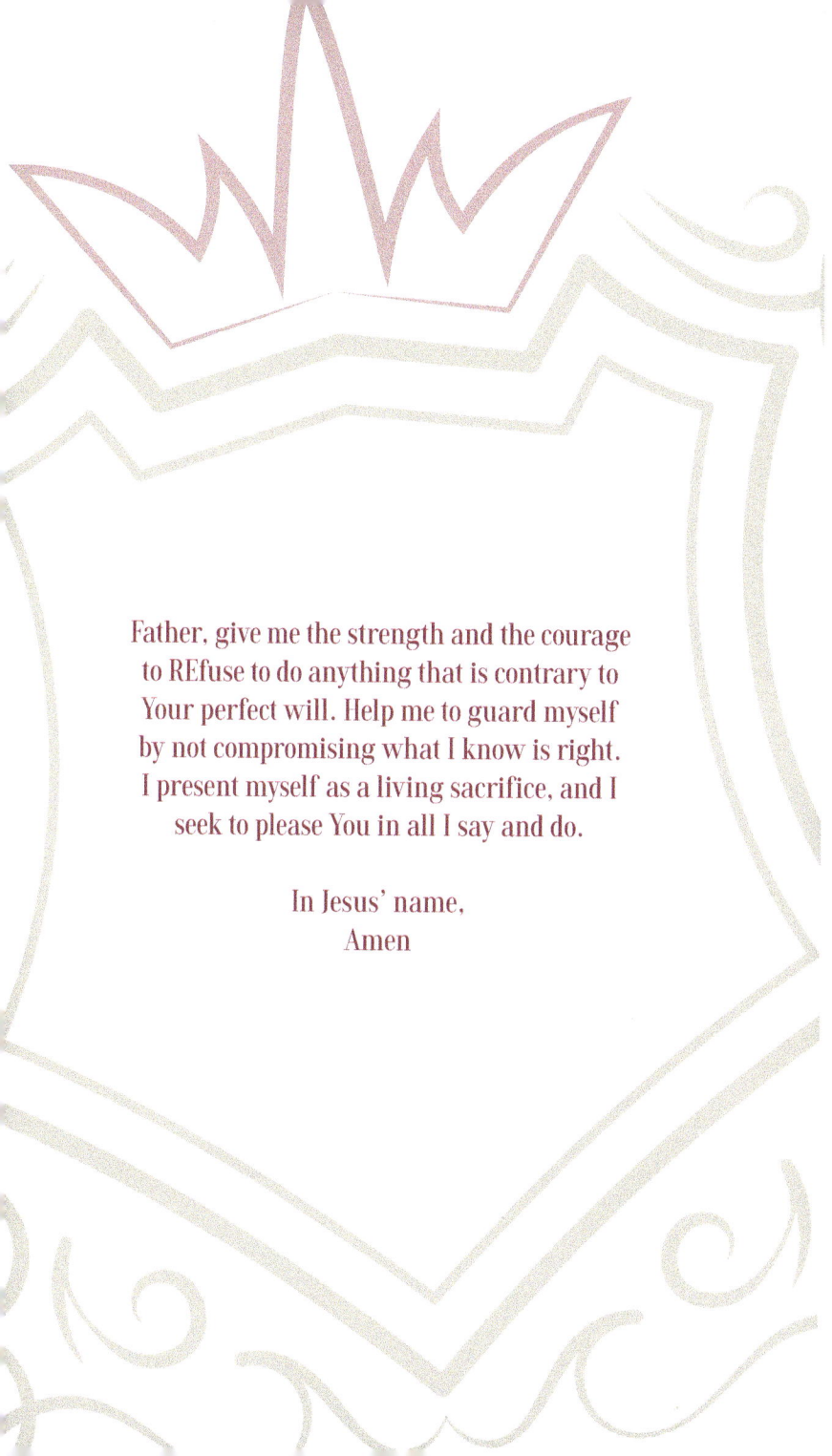

DAY 29

Ephesians 4:2-3

"Be completely humble and gentle; be patient, bearing with one another in love. Make every effort to keep the unity of the Spirit through the bond of peace."

THE POWER OF "RE"
RELATIONSHIP

When thinking about the word RElationship, the thought of sharing love and compassion with another immediately comes to mind. It simply means that you are connected by blood, marriage, business, or association. Strong and solid RElationships are to be desired, especially when all efforts are mutual.

In any RElationship, there should be mutual REspect for all parties involved. Husbands and wives should have mutual REspect and love for each other; friends should have mutual REspect and fondness; and business associates should have mutual REspect and aspirations. The problem with any RElationship is when the REspect, the love, the compassion, the effort, or the goal is not mutual.

The Bible teaches us in Ephesians that we are to be humble and gentle, to be patient bearing one another in love. When any elements of a healthy RElationship are missing, then RElationships become problematic. Unhealthy RElationships can potentially REsult in unhealthy people. RElationships are held together through the bond of peace. When the bond of peace is broken, there is nothing to hold the RElationship together and secure it. We cannot hold on to what has been broken, but there is no harm in evaluating where the bond was broken. James 3:16 says, "For where you have envy and selfish ambition, there you find disorder and every evil practice."

This is something to think about as you REcover from a RElationship that has been broken or is no longer salvageable. Even in these broken RElationships, you must always strive to live peaceably with everyone. You must strive to keep the bond of peace and be humble and gentle. And always REmember that a strong RElationship with our Lord and Savior takes precedence over any other RElationship you could ever involve yourself in.

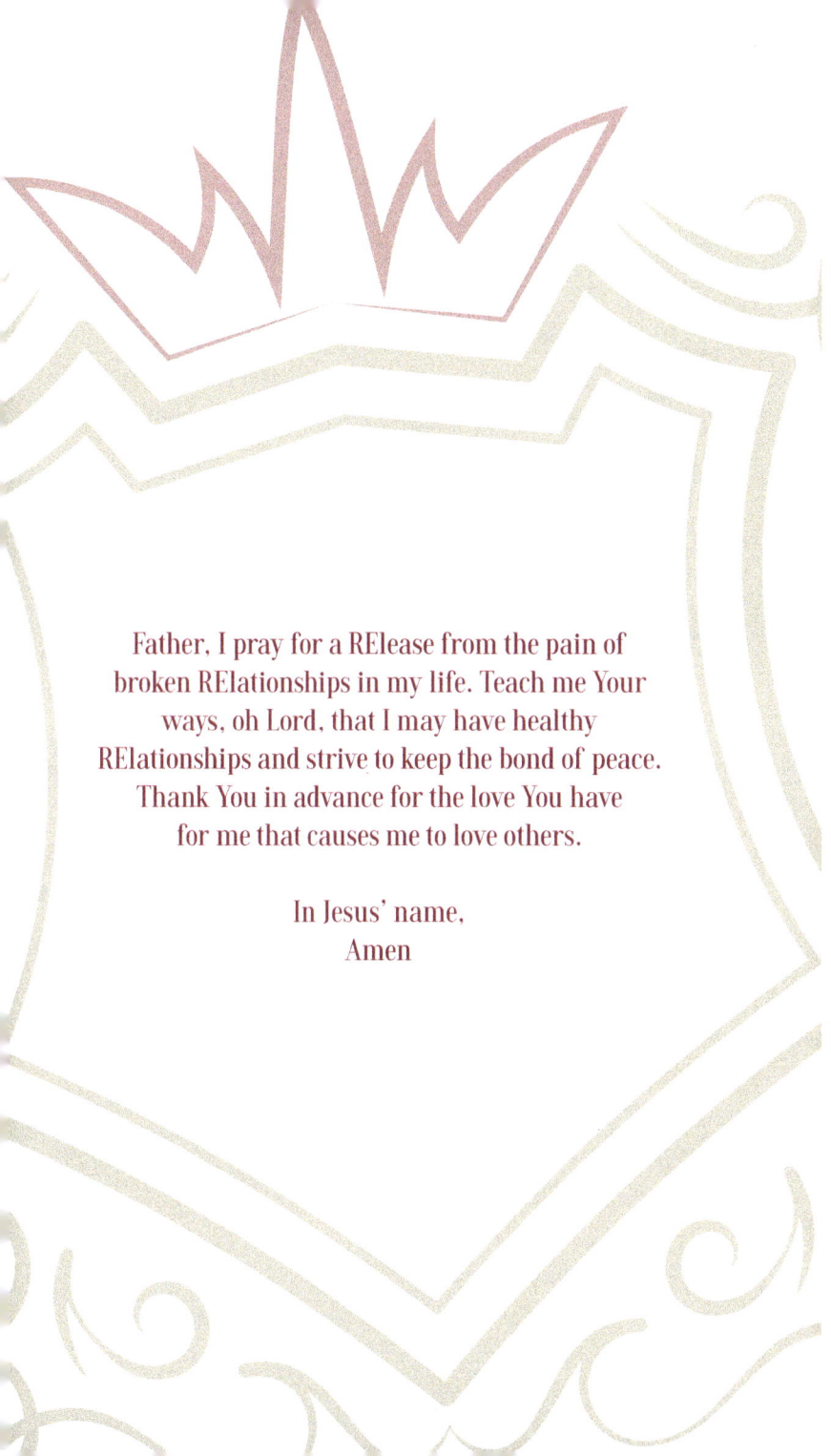

Father, I pray for a RElease from the pain of broken RElationships in my life. Teach me Your ways, oh Lord, that I may have healthy RElationships and strive to keep the bond of peace. Thank You in advance for the love You have for me that causes me to love others.

In Jesus' name,
Amen

DAY 30

Psalm 46:1-3

"God is our refuge and strength, an ever-present help in trouble. Therefore we will not fear, though the earth give way and the mountains fall into the heart of the sea, though its waters roar and foam and the mountains quake with their surging."

THE POWER OF "RE"
REFUGE

When we imagine a storm, we can visualize everything that makes it very difficult to navigate—the trees swaying back and forth, the tumultuous rain waters pouring down, the loud whistle of the winds. And sometimes, the only thing that comes to mind during this time is safety, shelter, a place of REfuge where the storm cannot harm us.

The storms of life are no different than the storms of nature. They are inevitable and nothing we intentionally plan for, and when they arise, they seem to catch us at unexpected moments—when things are going very well, when we have peace and happiness that seem unshakable and unbreakable. But then the unimaginable happens, and we find ourselves asking, "What do I do now?"

While we know nothing in life is certain nor is anything guaranteed to last until eternity, sometimes we find ourselves having a hard time processing and accepting what has happened. What we identify as being normal has been interrupted and is now in disarray. Beautiful families that once REpresented what a family should be are now torn apart; couples who were once labeled as power couples are now divorced and living separately. Our children who were once on the right path have now grown up and are living lives contrary to how they were raised. Finally, the job that not only provided necessities for living but also afforded a preferred lifestyle is no longer attainable.

These are just a few examples of storms and troubles in life. And with these types of storms, we need a safe place. We need a place where we can gather our thoughts to keep from losing our minds because of the pressure. We must understand that during these times we always have a place of REfuge in Jesus Christ. God is our REfuge (our safe place) and our strength (our power and our capacity to stand) even during the most boisterous storms. Not only is He our REfuge and our strength, but Psalm 46 says He is also an ever-present help in trouble.

In other words, there will never be a time that you are unsafe when you are enduring a storm. God is always there, even when it seems He is not. You must always REmember there is safety and protection found in the secret place of the Most High God. Where is this secret place? The secret place is within the presence of God, where all should dwell as His children.

Always REmember Psalm 91:1-2: "Whoever dwells in the shelter of the Most High will rest in the shadow of the Almighty. I will say of the Lord, 'He is my refuge and my fortress, my God, in whom I trust.'"

Father, thank You for being that secret place,
my REfuge and shelter from the storm.
Thank You for Your divine protection that has
always covered me and carried me through
the worst storms. I will forever dwell in the
secret place of the Most High God where I can rest
during my storms and find safety in times of trouble.

In Jesus' name,
Amen

DAY 31

Matthew 22:37-40

"Jesus replied: 'Love the Lord your God with all your heart and with all your soul and with all your mind.' This is the first and greatest commandment. And the second is like it: 'Love your neighbor as yourself.' All the Law and the Prophets hang on these two commandments."

THE POWER OF "RE"
REQUIREMENT

A REquirement is what is necessary or what it takes to obtain something great or something better than what we already have.

As followers of Christ, we know several REquirements are commanded of us. Matthew teaches us that we are to love the Lord our God with all our heart, soul, and mind and that we are to love our neighbor as we love ourselves. Hebrews 12:14 tells us to be holy because "without holiness no one will see the Lord." In other words, we are REquired to live by holy standards. Throughout the entire Bible, we can find what is necessary for us to REceive blessings from the Lord and for us to have eternal life.

REquirements are not only for our spiritual journey. We have REquirements at work, at home, at school, and in the marketplace. We should also have personal REquirements set forth in each of our individual lives, including when we form new RElationships and friendships. Understand, we are valuable; we have been fearfully and wonderfully made, (Psalm 139:14); we were created in the image of Christ, (Genesis 1:27); we are "a chosen generation, a royal priesthood, a holy nation, a God's special possession," (1 Peter 2:9). When we begin to understand our value and our worth, we will know the importance of establishing REquirements with people we allow to be in our inner circles.

Everyone should REquire loyalty, honesty, unconditional love, and REspect. When you have not established REquirements, then you will settle and accept anything people present to you. Now is a good time to stop discounting yourself and allowing people to mishandle the gift you are. REquire people to treat you the way royalty should be treated. You are a child of the Most High God, and you do not have to accept and settle for anything. REquire the best and enjoy the REsults.

Father, I thank You now that I know who I am and whose I am. Forgive me for allowing people to treat me less than what I am worth and mishandle me, the unique individual You have created me to be. As You REquire us to love, I will accept no less than that. Now that I understand my worth, I know that more should be REquired and expected. Thank You for this eye-opening moment.

In Jesus' name,
Amen

Notes

Notes

Notes

Notes

www.ingramcontent.com/pod-product-compliance
Lightning Source LLC
Chambersburg PA
CBHW050815090426
42736CB00021B/3456